CW01334488

PAK MEI
KUNG FU
(WHITE EYEBROW)

★

H. B. UN

PAUL H. CROMPTON LTD.
638 Fulham Road, London S.W.6. England

1st edition 1974

Copyright 1974 H. B. Un,
All rights reserved
Printed by Elsworth Bros. Ltd., Leeds LS10 1JD

長春警備司令。
新一軍軍長潘裕昆將軍

**GENERAL
PAN YU KUN, C.B.**
Commander of the
New First Army
Military Governor in Hanoi
(Second World War) and
Cheong Chun in
Manchuria

"Strong body, strong country" by the Most Honourable General Pan Yu Kun. Commander of the Chinese New First Army. Companion of the Order of the Bath of the British Empire

Mr. N. K. Ng,
Chairman of the
Hong Kong,
White Eyebrow,
Boxing Association.

武德重光

諸葛師傅奉書出版紀念

白眉國術總會
會長 伍角佳敬題

A revival of the
True spirit of
Martial Arts,
By Master N. K. Ng.

CONTENTS

About the Author	1
The Men of Pak Mei	3
Development of Pak Mei	12
First "Set" of Pak Mei	19
Advice to Kung Fu students	69
Examples of techniques	72

ABOUT THE AUTHOR

Mr. H. B. Un is a life long student of the Chinese Martial Arts which are generally called in the West: Kung Fu. He is also a teacher, and has a diploma of Arts and a Degree in Theology. In Hong Kong he was in charge of several large schools, one with 1500 students. When he was a child he suffered in common with many Chinese people from the effects of the Second World War. His health was impaired. He learned the Choy style of Kung Fu to try to improve his condition. Later he studied the Northern Praying Mantis style from the famous Master Wong Hon Fan 黃 漢 勛 one of the Sifu of the Hong Kong Ching Wu Athletic Association

香 港 精 武 體 育 會

After a long period he was deeply interested in Chinese Martial Arts and became one of the disciples of the Great Master Cheung Lai Chun 張 禮 泉

This Great Master was instructor of Kung Fu at the Chinese Wong Poe Military Academy. Master Cheung held eighteen Athletic Clubs in Canton under his control. Mr. Un is now the special reporter for the Chinese New Martial Hero magazine in England, Honourable Life Member of the Northern Praying Mantis style Hon Fun Athletic Association and Representative of the Hong Kong Pak Mei (White Eyebrow Style) Boxing Association in England.

He refused to teach Kung Fu in the London Chinese Youth Club and the Overseas Chinese Student Service Centre sponsored by the Chinese Methodist Church in London. This is the usual attitude of Chinese Kung Fu Sifu. They do not want to reveal any martial arts, personally, at all.

A portrait of White Eyebrow — The Taoist Sifu who founded the style and gave it his name

The Monk, Chuk Fat Wan, the Master of Master Cheung

Sifu Cheung Lai Chun, Kung Fu instructor of the Chinese Wong Poe Military Academy, in Taoist robes. Sifu Cheung studied the Taoist religion and obtained qulaifications in it.

Sifu Cheung on his 80th birthday

Master Cheung (seated) and Sifu D. Chan (r) Kung Fu instructor of the Chinese Laundry Association, New York, and the author

The author and Master Cheung and Sifu David K. Lee, General Executive Secretary of the Chinese Laundry Association, New York

Master Cheung (seated) and disciples
C. C. Liu, H. B. Un, Y. Mak, K. C. Chan, Y. Ng, S. H. Chan, N. K. Ng

White Eyebrow students who won the Taiwan Chinese Boxing Tournament in 1971, with their Sifu, N. K. Ng, White Eybrow students won the People's Republic of China Boxing Tournament, Mid-Southern Area, 1970

The author and the Great Master of Northern Praying Mantis style

Wong Hon Fan

北派螳螂宗師黃漢勛

The Development of the Pak Mei (White Eyebrow) Style in South China.

This is how it was told to me, H. B. Un, by my Master L. C. Cheung

Great Master Cheung Lai Chun was born in the Ching Dynasty. His great grandfather, Cheung Yok Tong was a Brigadier. During the time of the Emperor Ham Fung, Brigadier Cheung was one of the government officers in Kowloon Peninsular, Hong Kong. In 1859 the Brigadier built a monument in old Kowloon City and in the 9th year of the reign of the Emperor Ham Fung he built an old paper pavilion. People called it the Eight Corners Pavilion.

When Master Cheung was a baby his father died and his mother looked after him. When he was about four years old one of his dead father's cousins tried to encroach on the family property and acquire it solely for himself. He threw the tiny Master Cheung into a thorn bush and broke his left arm. The child was taken to a Chinese surgeon called Sifu Lam Shek, nicknamed Smallpox Lam. Sifu Lam healed his left arm. After some years, at the age of seven, Master Cheung became one of his students and learned from him Gipsy style. He also learned the Cross Set (Kata), Sun, Moon, Monkey, Knife and other Sets. Later Master Cheung became a student of Sifu Lee Mung, the son of a famous Sifu called Lee Yee. He learned the Seventy-Two Earth Ghosts Set, Group Fighting Stick Set, Snake Hidden in a Stream Stick Set, Five Elements Central Stick Set, Left and Right Big Hayfork Set, Single Knife and Shield Set, and many others.

Later, an uncle on his mother's side brought him to the Wah Sau Temple in Lor Fow Mountain and he became a student of the Great Master Lam Ah-Hap. Before this he had learned Dragon Style from Sifu Wong Che Si and Sifu Lam Ah Yuan, father of the Great master Lam Yue Quai, instructor of Kung Fu at the Yin Tong Military Academy. Sifu Lam Ah-Hap was a student of the famous Tai Yok Monk. All these Sifus were Dragon Style. They taught the Dragon Sets Dragon

Depressing Hand Set, Serpent Hiss Set, Single Knife and Single Horse Set, and so forth. This style of Kung Fu is a very fierce style. Master Lam Yue Quai practised only this style and he became an expert in it.

The fist attacks are fierce and quick and the movements kept in close to the body. All the body moves in a lively way in this style. Master Lam Yue Quai used a hammer fist blow to beat Mr. C. K. Lai in a contest, the bodyguard of the Governor of the Kwantung Province, His Excellency C. T. Chan,

When Master Cheung controlled 18 Athletic Clubs in Canton he put this style into his intermediate course. The special points of this style are to put the rear hand by the side of the front hand, use the sheep step, and leech movement.

Later, Master Lam Yue Quai and Master Cheung Lai Chun went to Canton and tried their luck. Every morning Master Cheung went to a teahouse and had his breakfast. One morning he saw a young monk enjoying himself in the teahouse. At that time, Manchurians still had a big influence in Canton. They were descendants of Manchurian Army Officers. They were cruel and arrogant people but not one of them dared to join the table of this young monk. After several days of observation Master Cheung decided that the young monk was an unusual person, otherwise the Manchurians would not have been intimidated into staying away from his table. When Master Cheung sat down at the table the young monk got up and walked away; this happened repeatedly. At last Master Cheung spoke to the young monk:

"Sifu, I am not a leper. For what reason do you walk away from me? We are both Chinese!"

The young monk thought for a while then sat down with him. After several weeks they became friends. One day, on the birthday of a certain god, Master Cheung prepared some food and invited the young monk to be his guest. They also drank, and the young monk became a little tipsy. Master Cheung tried to talk to him about Kung Fu. But the young monk just kept on eating and said nothing. At length, Master Cheung spoke.

"Sifu, may I give a performance of my Kung Fu knowledge?" Then Master Cheung performed a certain Kata or Set.

"Do you think it is good enough for real fighting?" he asked the monk. The monk replied non-committally, "It depends."

Master Cheung said, "Ah, Sifu, you know Kung Fu, otherwise you would not talk to me like this. Will you please give a demonstration then we can see something."

The young monk was still tipsy. He stood up and gave a performance of three movements of the Set Kou Po Teaw (Nine Step Push). He showed one spearhand technique, one Phoenix eye punch and one Monk-Takes-Off-Robe. Then he stopped. Master Cheung criticised him unfavourably.

"Sifu, your Kung Fu is not useful. You just stood there. How can you hit your opponent like that?"

The young monk said, "It depends." He meant that it depended on what sort of opponent you met. Then Cheung said, "Maybe we can have a private contest." The young monk said nothing but just stood there. Reluctantly Cheung asked him to put himself on guard. The monk just shook his head. Cheung rushed forward and used an arrow fist from the Lee style to attack him. Then he retreated and tried to slip to the right hand side of the monk. But the monk blocked his arm, and stopped him. Cheung tried to use some other techniques but could not make any headway. Then he said, "Let's try again, I still have some other movements left." Soon after, he told me, he used the Dragon style called After Three Drums Prepare to Cross the Bridge, rushed, deflected and tried to make the monk block him. Then he used the Close Ear and Shoulder movement to make him fall. Unfortunately for Master Cheung the young monk used the technique he had earlier shown: Monk Takes Off Robe. He turned at the waist, blocked and pushed. The Master Cheung flew off like an aeroplane descending to the airport. As he flew down he landed on a goldfish tank, and broke it.

He was cut on the chin by broken glass and seriously shocked. He got up, not understanding why he had been flung away by this little monk so easily. Blood came from his chin. He sighed and spoke with the monk.

"Ah, Great Monk, if you had shown me your real art I would not have dared to challenge you. May I have the honour of becoming your student?" The monk waved his hands and said, "I could never do this; if my Sifu were to hear of it he would think that I was showing off here, there and everywhere and I would be punished." Cheung felt astonished.

"My lord, your Kung Fu is so marvellous, your Sifu must be very, very good. Come on, introduce me to him." This request made the young monk nervous. He said, "Please be kind enough not to try to see my Sifu." He went on, "If he knew that I had showed somebody my Kung Fu he would half kill me." At that time Cheung did not insist on seeing his Sifu. He just made friends with this young monk and invited him out to meals as usual. After several weeks he had gleaned that the old Sifu of the monk was called Chuk Fat Wan. His favourite and almost exclusive food was eggs. He was then living in Kwong How Temple, Canton.

It transpired that old Chuk Fat Wan had been a disciple at a Taoist temple where Pak Mei, the Taoist Priest, had taught his students, in the Kwang Wai Temple of Sze Chuan Province. When Chuk Fat Wan had completed his training he had brought his disciple Lin Sang to visit some other provinces of China. When he arrived in Canton he had taken up residence in Kwong How Temple. He was then 92 years old. At that same time Master Cheung had completed his own training in Lee style, Gipsy style, and Dragon style. He had thought that he was an excellent boxer, and was trying his luck in Canton. Having been beaten by the young monk his confidence had been shown to be ill-founded. He showed me, the author, his chin and said to me.

"This is my scar, my testimony, of learning Pak Mei Kung Fu." Continuing with his story Master Cheung related how one day he had bought two large baskets of eggs and followed the young monk Lin Sang to the Kwong How Temple. This quite annoyed the young monk, but master Cheung ignored his displeasure. When they met Chuk Fat Wan the old Master was angry. The young monk knelt down on the floor and bowed to his Master. Master Cheung explained that he was looking for the true martial arts. Sincerely he wanted to become a disciple. Old Sifu Chuk refused him. He told Cheung he would leave Canton and go to another place, but Master Cheung said that he would follow him. At last he was accepted and he sold some fields and other property and followed the old Sifu. After three years the old Sifu taught Cheung Kou Po Teaw Set, Eighteen Deflect with Palm Set, Fierce-Tiger-Comes-Out-From-The-Forest Set, Double Flying Phoenix Knives, Tonfas, and other methods. Master Cheung then became the first man to introduce the Pak Mei style into South China.

Master Cheung not only excelled in Kung Fu but also in Chinese herbal medicine, bone-setting and such, meditation, making the body impervious to pain. During the rebellion to overthrow the Ching dynasty he took part in the famous battle called "March 29". Once he was a captain of Mr. W. F. Lau's army. In the third year of the Republic of China he took part in a duel with Mr. Wong, the general Kung Fu instructor of the Black Flag Army. He was highly praised. He beat a famous Sifu called H. C. Yip and Mr. S. P. Woo, disciple of a famous Iron Arm Sifu. In the 5th Year of the Republic he beat the Iron Head Monk of the Hoi Tung Temple, Canton. He went to Kwong Mon to carry on a salt business and was attacked by hooligans with daggers. He was surrounded once by a crowd of 60 or so hooligans and hit and hunted down more than 20 of them.

Later he returned to his own country and helped a man called Ah Geng to open a Kung Fu club in Pai Mei village Wai Chow. Then he went to Sun Wai District to teach Kung Fu there. He beat a muscle man type boxer called Mr. S. Chan. He went to Toi San District and stayed there for two years. After several years he returned to Canton and opened eighteen Kung Fu clubs there.

Pak Mei style is in between inner and Outer styles. It is difficult for beginners to appreciate and learn it. Not many people have enough patience to learn it.

Once Master Cheung was instructor of the family of his Excellency C. T. Chan, Governor of Kwantung Province and one of the instructors of the Wong Poe Military Academy. During the Second World War after several careful selections the academy adopted three bayonet techniques from Master Cheung's repertoire.

In 1949 Master Cheung retired and went to Hong Kong with two of his sons. He opened a Chinese herbal shop called Po War Tong in Ki Lung Street. This was in the Sham Shiu Po District, Kowloon Peninsula. He was not a businessman. His shop closed down later. In Hong Kong he only accepted a few people to become his disciples. Some of these disciples are Sifu of other styles of Kung Fu or had studied other styles before. In Fan Ling, New Territory Hong Kong there was a Justice of the Peace called Mr. C. C. Lee. He invited Master Cheung to teach his village young men and Mr. F. T. Lee, one of the very famous Sifu of the Lee style in Sah Tou Kok Area, New Territory, invited Master Cheung to teach him and his village men. At one time not many people in Hong Kong knew Pak Mei style because Master Cheung did not allow his disciples to teach, to take part in tournaments or show off or give performances.

In 1961 Master Cheung still had no grey hairs and no wrinkles on his hands. He kept his standard of Kung Fu at the age of eighty. One year, he gave a performance for charity in a huge amusement park, and hundreds of Sifu from other styles came to see his demonstration. All of them were astonished that Master Cheung kept his Kung Fu standard and was so superb. He smoked more than 40 cigarettes a day at this time and ate very little. He grew worse in health and did not accept advice from his students. He passed away in the autumn of 1964 at the age of 84.

In 1970 students of Pak Mei won the Championships of the Middle Southern Area of the People's Republic of China. In 1971 students of Pak Mei won two championships in Taiwan. Now there are more than 50 Kung Fu clubs under the name of Hong Kong Pak Mei Boxing Association.

Author's and Publisher's Note

After some deliberations Mr. H. B. Un and Mr. P. H. Crompton decided that although the photographs in existence of Master Cheung were not of a high standard, and although some of them were missing, it was preferable to use photographs of the great Master of Pak Mei, both in his honour as a Master of Kung Fu, and so that students of Kung Fu should have a visual record of a man whose like is rapidly diminishing in the modern world. Some essential photographs have been taken of Mr. H. B. Un to fill in the gaps. So it is without apologies that the following presentation of Kou Po Teaw (Nine Step Push) is made. Master Cheung was 79 years of age when these photographs were taken.

THE FIRST 'SET' OF
PAK MEI (WHITE EYEBROW) KUNG FU
(Gou Boo Teaw — Nine Step Push)

This style of Kung Fu is a combination of 'inner' and 'outer' approaches. It is not completely 'inner' or 'soft' like Tai Chi Chuan, nor 'outer' and 'hard' like Hung Gar (?).

Pak Mei contains something of the Taoist idea of Yin and Yang, the Female and Male principles: opposites whose balance within a living creature or system maintains that creature or system in a state of harmony.

Breathing is important in Pak Mei but it is not advisable to try and convey the breathing method in a book; it must really be learned from a competent teacher.

The 'compass' diagram shown on p.19 is the same as was used in Mr. Un's first volume in this series, 'Praying Mantis' kung fu. The 'Set' starts from a position of facing North, and subsequent movements are described in relation to this initial position.

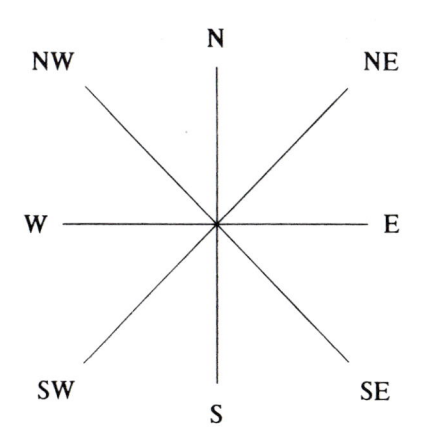

1. Face N. in position shown in Fig 1. The open right palm heel rests upon the upright clenched left fist. The fist is lightly clenched. Take the two hands, in the same position, up to the left shoulder, across the left side of the chest and so to the middle of the body, near the chin. Then down to the solar plexus and then out to the first position.

1A The right hand bends forward from the wrist in a Crane 'fist,' at the side of the clenched left fist. The right fingers circle under the left fist and then the fingers open palm upwards. As the right fingers open into an upwards facing palm the left fist opens into a downward facing palm. At this point, whilst the palms are opening, step forward North with the left foot. Extend both arms horizontally forward with the right open palm still facing up and the left facing down. Weight is evenly distributed on both feet. Fig. 2.

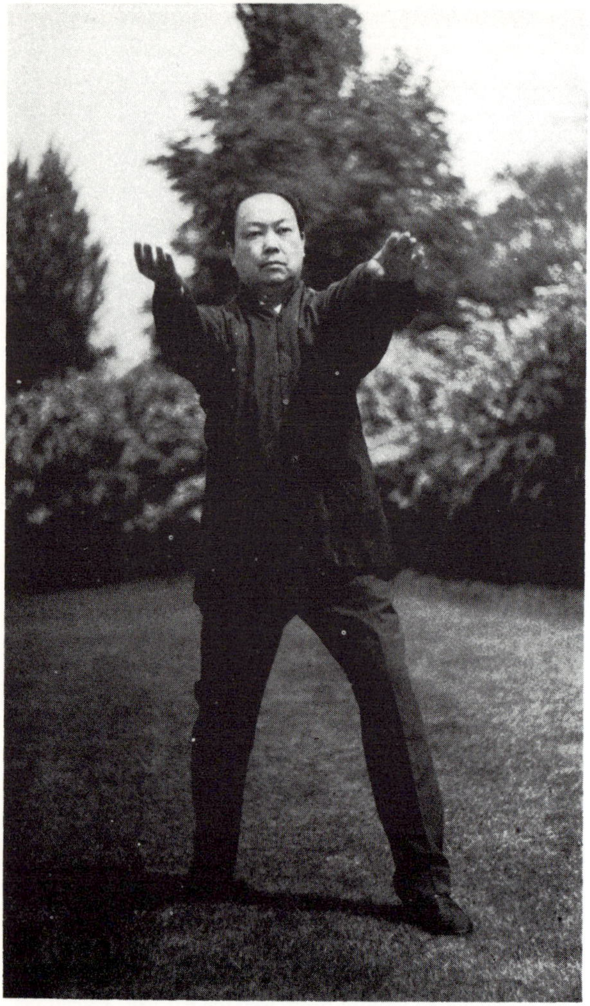

3. The right arm draws back, bending at the elbow to an angle of about 100 degrees, forming a fist, palm up. At the same time the left open palm presses downwards to about abdomen level, again also drawing back a little by bending at the elbow. The 'depressing' movement of the left palm flows into a forward thrust with the extended fingers. Note; these movements are smooth, even, flowing and unhurried. This is not a 'hard,' muscle-tensing 'set.'

4. The left hand draws back to form a similar fist to the right hand, and the right hand extends in a downward facing fist, with the knuckle of the first finger extended beyond the closed fist in the single Phoenix eye.

5. Open the right hand facing down. Step forward with the left foot followed immediately by the right. Same stance and weight distribution as before. Left hand opens and at same time: right hand draws back, palm down, to near left shoulder and left hand draws back palm up to under right armpit. Right hand turns palm up and then both palms cross one another as they extend forward in a 'push' type of movement ending in the formation of Tiger Claws.

6. Clench fists and turn to face upwards turning both arms out a fraction from the elbow.

7. Open both fists and 'push' forwards horizontally extending arms. Palms vertical.

8. Form fists with both hands palm upwards and draw back arms to position shown, Like No. 6.

9. Turn both feet East simultaneously, taking the right arm extended horizontally, palm down, East also, as the trunk follows the feet. The left palm, facing up, travels with the right arm, but below it and closer in to the body, as if holding a ball, i.e. a big ball.

10. Re-adjust the left foot by moving it a little. The right hand turns to form an upward facing fist, bending at the elbow, and the left moves close to the right elbow, vertical open palm, as if 'covering' the elbow, but not touching it.

11. As the right arm moves fractionally outwards, the left hand pushes forward, palm down, fingers straight and together.

12. Open the right hand, palm up. The left and right hands move simultaneously. Right comes back to under left armpit and left comes back above it, palm down, to right shoulder. Both arms re-cross and push forward, finally forming Tiger Claws, and the right and left feet step forward, right-left as the push is made. When the Tiger Claws are made the right hand is just ahead and above the left.

13. Open the Tiger Claws, turn both palms to face the body, the right hand being nearer the body, the left palm close behind it. Turn both palms inwards and then push forwards to form Tiger Claws. This time the left hand is ahead of and slightly above the right. Step forward again.

14. Open the right hand, palm up. The left and right hands move simultaneously. Right comes back to under left armpit and left comes back above it, palm down, to right shoulder. Both arms re-cross and push forward, finally forming Tiger Claws, and the right and left feet step forward, right-left as the push is made. When the Tiger Claws are made the right hand is just ahead and above the left. Step forward again.

15. Re-adjust the left foot by moving it a little. The right hand turns to form an upward facing fist, bending at the elbow, and the left moves close to the right elbow, vertical open palm, as if 'covering' the elbow, but not touching it.

16. Turn North from waist, opening hands as shown, then swing back East keeping same hand position.

17. Re-adjust the left foot by moving it a little. The right hand turns to form an upward facing fist, bending at the elbow, and the left moves close to the right elbow, vertical open palm, as if 'covering' the elbow, but not touching it.

18. Turn left at the waist and as you turn step North with the right foot, so that the whole body turns 180 degrees. Place the right foot facing West. Take the left foot to join the right then immediately step West with the left foot. The hand positions remain the same, until the left foot steps West. The left hand follows the left foot, palm down extending West.

19. Left hand draws back into fist palm up. Right hand makes Phoenix eye punch.

20. Step West with left foot and right at same time withdraw right fist a few inches, open hand and push palm forward. Draw back right palm, downwards to left shoulder, left palm up to right armpit and as right reaches shoulder palm turns upwards facing. Hands cross and separate, then push forwards to form Tiger Claws.

21. Open palms, lower hands from wrists, rotate at wrist to form upward facing fists, arms bent about 100 deg. Like No. 6.

22. Open hands, rotate inwards from wrists, and push both forwards. Like No. 7.

23. Form fists, palm upwards, drawing back arms to about 100 deg.

24. Turn both feet North, open palms, rotate down and up from wrists. Body also is now facing North, and hands push forwards; the right goes horizontally forward, and the left goes down away from the body in front of the genitals.

25. Right hand forms fist, and palm up moves slightly back and out to the right. At same time the left palm goes up and forward palm facing down, then comes back to form same fist and position as right. At the same time as the left comes back into a fist the right thrusts forward open palm down. Repeat with the left forward and right forming fist then repeat with right forward and left forming fist.

26. Left foot comes close to right and then steps out and North. At the same time the right palm comes back, palm down to the left shoulder and the left palm face up to right armpit. Cross back over with right palm up and push to form Tiger Claw. Left ahead and slightly above right.

27. Left and right step forward. Open Tiger Claws and turn palms to face body. Right hand passes under and ahead of left, push to form Tiger Claws again.

28. Left foot comes close to right and then steps out and North. At the same time the right palm comes back, palm down to the left shoulder and the left palm face up to right armpit. Cross back over with right palm up and push to form Tiger Claw. Left ahead and slightly above right.

29 Left and right step forward. Open Tiger Claws and turn palms to face body. Right hand passes under and ahead of left, push to form Tiger Claws again.

30. Right hand rotates into a fist, palm up. The left forms a fist palm down and 'blocks' over the top of it, as if defending against a punch to the waist then moves out and up palm up, so that you are in a position or 'guard' similar to the old prize fighters. Take the weight on the front, left foot and kick using the outer edge of the right foot, low, across the body.

31.

32. After the kick the right foot steps North. The right arm, palm open facing vertically inwards swings to the right, fingers and arm pointing North. The left arm swings with it, in the same direction and position but slightly back from the right and bent at the elbow.
(Vertical: i.e. The palm in a vertical plane.)

33. The right hand draws back into a fist, palm up facing and the left comes in close to the right elbow open palm, as if guarding the elbow.

34. The right hand makes a 'grasping' fist (Emperor offers you a glass of wine) as if holding a tumbler of wine in your hand: left hand does the same. The right hand is held vertically above the left and the right rises as the left sinks. To explain this more clearly: imagine you grasped a pole with both hands. The right hand slides up the pole and the left slides down it. As the hand movement is made the left leg is raised from the knee and bends up at the side of the right. Lower leg is horizontally held.

m. Opponent starts kick. Defender ready

n. Defender catches at ankle between thumb and index finger

o. Turning left the defender thrusts forward

79

p. Punch at abdomen

80 q. Chop down and counter punch

r. Block and lean head away

s. Counter open finger thrust

81

35. Step back South with left foot, draw right foot to it, step back South with left foot again, right foot steps back, across and in front of left foot, i.e. legs are crossed, right in front of left. The hands stay the same.

36. As the legs cross, turn the body to the left, East, turning the feet East also. The right hand, palm up, comes over and crosses the left hand, also palm up, at waist level at the same time as the body continues to turn so that it faces North East. In other words, you make a 270 degree turn with feet and body, from North, through West, to East, and the body from the waist continues to move with the hands to North East. Then, turn the body back to face East.

37. The hands separate and push out and up till they point horizontally sideways.

38. Turn again trunk North, crossing hands as in No. 36.

39. Step across the front of the body, North, with the right foot, to face West. The left foot joins the right and then immediately steps West. As the left foot steps West, just as it reaches the ground, the left hand palm down thrusts forward, open, and the right blocks outwards, fist clenched upwards.

40. Left fist does same as right in move 39 and right punches forward Phoenix-eye punch.

41. Right fist opens, arm retracts slightly and push forward. Left foot steps forward. Left arm remains same. Right arm continues its movement palm down and comes back as before to left shoulder, left back to right armpit, palm down. Hands re-cross, separating, and push forward to form Tiger Claws.

Step West with left foot and right at same time withdraw right fist a few inches, open hand and push palm forward. Draw back right palm, downwards to left shoulder, left palm up to right armpit and as right reaches shoulder palm turns upwards facing. Hands cross and separate, then push forwards to form Tiger Claws.

42. Retract claws to form fists, palms up.

43. Rotate open palms at wrists and push out both palms.

44. Again form fists, palm up, bending the arms slightly and thus drawing the fists back and outwards.

45 Turn North, right foot in front. Right palm down the right arm extends horizontally forward, whilst left palm presses down, defending groin.

46. Let hands go down from wrists then form Tiger Claws as hands both draw back to close to left hip.

47. Move the left foot to the right. Hands take position of No. 1 move.

48. Face N. in position shown in Fig 1. The open right palm heel rests upon the upright clenched left fist. The fist is lightly clenched. Take the two hands, in the same position up to the left shoulder, across the left side of the chest and so to the middle of the body, near the chin. Then down to the solar plexus and then out to the first position.
Termination of Pak Mei, Nine Step Push Set, Gou Boo Teaw.

ADVICE TO KUNG FU STUDENTS

We all wish that our country and our countrymen should be prosperous and strong, civilised and healthy. The way to reach these goals is to improve ourselves physically through Kung Fu, sports, athletics, and so on. This will produce a fit, strong, and healthy people. For the country itself to flourish it must develop its agriculture. its industry and its cultural life.

The Chinese martial arts which are generally called in the West by the name of 'Kung Fu' have spread in popularity through South East Asia, Europe and America. However, according to my humble observation and opinion there are not many books and magazines for sound reference to these topics. Some of the books I have seen do not give the reader a clear idea of Kung Fu. Kung Fu includes physical training, as well as self defence.

Kung Fu involves the use of the fingers, palms, hands, elbows, shoulders, body or trunk, arms, knees and feet for attack and defence. Weapons also are included in Kung Fu: halberd, spear, sword, knife, axe, hay fork, stick, bench, bow and arrow, hammer, tonfa, hooks, etc.

In addition, it includes medicine, herbal healing, vital points attack as in the principles of acupuncture, judo, wrestling, Chinese Yoga, meditation, spiritual training and the study of longevity.

The words 'Kung Fu' mean: 1/ practice more, and 2/ martial arts. The Chinese character 武 (wu-martial arts) means "stop fighting". The main purpose of Kung Fu is to strengthen oneself to protect others and defend one's country. After you have studied Kung Fu for a time you realise that it is not good to fight, and it is also very dangerous to fight.

There are many different styles of Kung Fu. The basic movements were mostly adapted from the movements of animals: dragon, snake, tiger, leopard, crane, lion, chicken, duck, swallow, eagle, mouse, bear, praying mantis, lamb, turtle, and so on. Some styles are suitable for physical training, some for younger people, some for elderly people and some for women.

It is employed as a physical exercise to help the circulation of the blood, develop the figure, stretch the joints and deepen the breathing. The weight of the body can also change and certain diseases can be avoided through the training in Kung Fu.

When you start to study Kung Fu you should remember certain principles.

a. Train in the morning from ten minutes to one hour. If you are busy in the morning then try mid-day or in the evening. Never after a meal.

b. You can use your back garden, balcony, a park, your room or club. It makes no difference.

c. Practise for several minutes then rest for a few minutes. Never make yourself too tired. After you have finished do not sit down or stand still but walk about slowly until your breath is back to normal. Sleep early if possible.

d. To help your concentration, avoid noise, do not eat, do not talk or laugh during training. Do not drink iced drinks after training.

e. Always try to breathe through the nose, and do not stand about in the cold if you have been sweating during practise.

f. Wear a shirt or uniform which is clean. Do not train in dirty clothes. Have some respect for your art. You should respect yourself and your instructor and your fellow students. Try to avoid getting hurt and hurting another.

g. According to the Shaolin (Sil-lum) Temple teaching, sexual intercourse should be avoided three days before and four days after hard training.

h. Remember there is no magic in Kung Fu. Do not expect to become a great master in a very short time.

Pak Mei (White Eyebrow) style is between internal style and external style. It is based on principles of physiology, psychology, dynamics, self defence, promoting good health and seeking longevity. This style of Chinese Boxing does not use brute force. You may think that this Set (Kata, Sequence of Movements) is too short and too simple.

After a long period of continual practise you will feel that intrinsic energy is developed. Pay attention in all movements. Make them slow and even. Ensure that head, neck, waist, stomach, hands, feet and knees are in the right position. The head is straight and natural, the spinal column stands in a normal line, the chest rests naturally, the shoulders remain lowered, breathing is smooth and always through the nose.

By following this advice you develop what in Aikido is called 'Ki.' Some diseases can be alleviated by right study of this.

I cordially invite the reader to remember that Kung Fu is not only for self defence. It has some interest for people who like to study movement and can open the mind to new experiences. It is a subtle system of the Chinese philosophy of life. This latter point is the most important in Chinese Kung Fu and is not easily understood by beginners.

a. Draw back from fist attack

b. Grab wrist and neck, or collar

c. Parry punch attack

d. Counter to solar plexus region

e. Your wrist is grabbed

f. Draw back right arm, thrusting up with left as shown

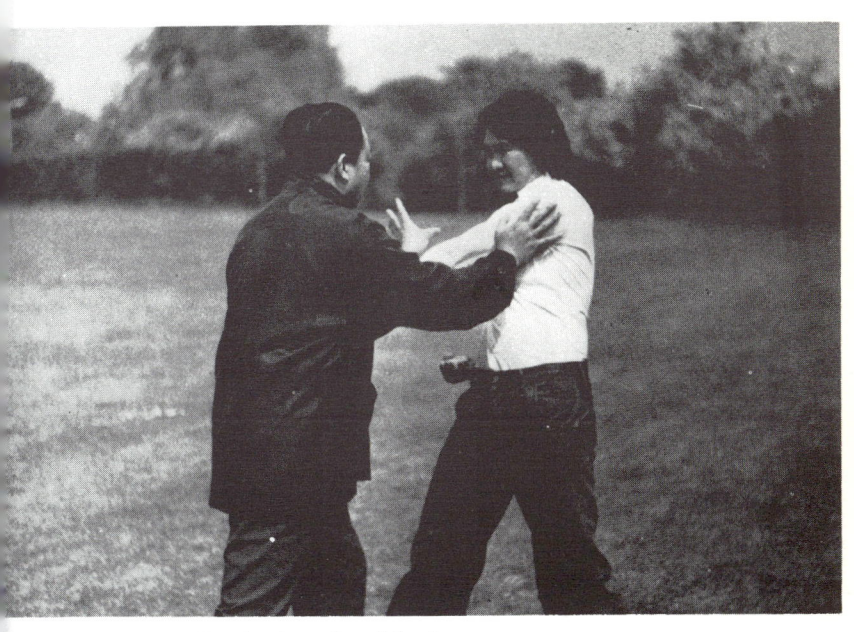

g. Break grip, and push hard

h. Opponent attacks as shown. Block and turn

i. Seize his left wrist, and upper arm

j. Pull forward. Opponent is open to further blows

k. Block as shown

l. Depress with left and punch